Smoothies for Diab

13th Edition

By Don Orwell

http://SuperfoodsToday.c...

D1503588

Your Free Gift

As a way of saying thanks for your purchase, I'm offering you my FREE eBook that is exclusive to my book and blog readers.

Superfoods Cookbook - Book Two has over 70 Superfoods recipes and complements Superfoods Cookbook Book One and it contains Superfoods Salads, Superfoods Smoothies and Superfoods Deserts with ultra-healthy non-refined ingredients. All ingredients are 100% Superfoods.

It also contains Superfoods Reference book which is organized by Superfoods (more than 60 of them, with the list of their benefits), Superfoods spices, all vitamins, minerals and antioxidants. Superfoods Reference Book lists Superfoods that can help with 12 diseases and 9 types of cancer.

http://www.SuperfoodsToday.com/FREE

Table of Contents

Smoothies for Diabetics Introduction

Hello,

My name is Don Orwell, and my blog SuperfoodsToday.com is dedicated to Superfoods lifestyle. I was able to lose 80 pounds in 2009 and keep them off by eating only regular everyday Superfoods. After several Superfoods related books, I decided to write one about smoothies for diabetics. I hope you will enjoy the recipes I prepared for you. Recipes have only ingredients listed and instructions how to blend a perfect smoothie are given here as a short introduction:

Put the liquid in first. Surrounded by tea or yogurt, the blender blades can move freely. Next, add chunks of fruits or vegetables. Leafy greens are going into the pitcher last. Preferred liquid is green tea, but you can use almond or coconut milk or herbal tea.

Start slow. If your blender has speeds, start it on low to break up big pieces of fruit. Continue blending until you get a puree. If your blender can pulse, pulse a few times before switching to a puree mode. Once you have your liquid and fruit pureed, start adding greens, very slowly. Wait until previous batch of greens has been completely blended. I use blenders because they're sturdy and offer 7 year warranty. That was definitely the best investment in my health.

Thicken? Added too much tea or coconut milk? Thicken your smoothie by adding ice cubes, flax meal, chia seeds or oatmeal. Once you get used to various tastes of smoothies, add any seaweed, spirulina, chlorella powder or ginger for additional kick. Experiment with any Superfoods in powder form at this point. Think of adding any nut butter or sesame paste too or some Superfoods oils.

Rotate! Rotate your greens; don't always drink the same smoothie! At the beginning try 2 different greens every week and later introduce third and fourth one weekly. And keep rotating them. Don't use spinach and kale all the time. Try beets greens, they have a pinch of pink in them and that add great color to your smoothie. Here is the list of leafy green for you to try: spinach, kale, dandelion, chards, beet leaves, arugula, lettuce, collard greens, bok choy, cabbage, cilantro, parsley.

Flavor! Flavor smoothies with ground vanilla bean, cinnamon, ½ tsp. of lucuma powder, nutmeg, cloves, almond butter, cayenne pepper, ginger or just about any seeds or chopped nuts combination.

Not only are green smoothies high in nutrients, vitamins and fiber, they can also make any vegetable you probably don't like (be it kale, spinach or broccoli) taste great. The secret behind blending the perfect smoothie is using sweet fruits or nuts or seeds to give your drink a unique taste.

There's a reason kale and spinach seem to be the main ingredients in almost every green smoothie. Not only do they give smoothies their verdant color, they are also packed with calcium, protein and iron.

Although blending alone increases the accessibility of carotenoids, since the presence of fats is known to increase carotenoid absorption from leafy greens, it is possible that coconut oil, nuts and seeds in a smoothie could increase absorption further.

Fruits and Veggies preparation

• Wash fruits and veggies

• Pluck leaves and stems from berries

• Core apples (optional)

• Peel orange, lemon, lime, grapefruit, kiwi, beet, pomegranate, ginger, dragon fruit and banana

• Peel and take the seeds out of papaya

• Remove seeds from peppers, apricots, peaches, cherries, plums and prunes

• Mangos, melons and avocados should be peeled, and inner seed taken out

• Watermelons should have their outer rind removed.

• Scoop out the flesh from passion fruit

• Cut fruits and veggies in 2-inch slices

If you can't find some ingredient, replace it with the closest one.

All details about each ingredient (vitamins, minerals, antioxidants etc.) can be found in my free Superfoods Reference book:
http://superfoodstoday.com/Free

RED SMOOTHIES

Carrot Ginger Smoothie

2 Carrots

2 Apples

1 cup of crushed ice

Pinch of nutmeg

½ tsp. Cinnamon

1 tbsp. Minced ginger

Spinach Berries Smoothie

- ½ cup almond milk
- ½ cup water
- 1 carrot
- 1 cup spinach
- 1 cup frozen raspberries
- 1 tablespoon Chia seeds
- 1 tablespoon fresh mint
- ½ teaspoon Lucuma powder

Strawberry Carrot Smoothie

- 1 cup frozen strawberries

- 1 banana

- 1 carrot

- 1 cup crushed ice

- 2 tablespoons Hemp seeds

- 1 tsp. Fresh Mint

Red Peppers Tomato Salad Smoothie

1 cup Red Peppers

1/2 medium avocado

2 medium tomatoes

1 cucumber

2 tablespoons lemon juice

1 tsp. olive oil & 1 tsp. chopped garlic

Pinch of sea salt & 1 tbsp. dill

1/2 cup crushed ice

Apricots & Carrots Smoothie

4 apricots

1 apple

1 cup red spinach

2 carrots

1 cup water

1 tbsp. Maca

Strawberries Yogurt Smoothie

- 1 cup strawberries

- ½ cup low-fat plain yogurt

- 3 ice cubes

- 1 tbsp. Ground coconut

- 1 tbsp. Acai

Red Swiss Smoothie

- 1 cup Red Swiss chard

- ½ cup raspberries, frozen

- 1/2 cup peaches, frozen

- 1 tbsp. Pumpkin seeds

- 1 orange

- 1 cup crushed ice

Red Leaf Lettuce Smoothie

- 1 cup Red Leaf Lettuce

- 1 Bananas

- 1 Celery stalk

- 1/2 cup Strawberry

- 1/2 cup Raspberry

- 1 cup crushed ice

- 1 clove & pinch of nutmeg

Red Veggie Smoothie

- 1 cup chopped tomato

- 1 kiwi

- 1 banana

- 1/2 celery stalk

- 1/4 cup each cilantro and spinach

- 1 tbsp. Olive oil

- Pinch of sea salt

- 1/2 cup ice

Papaya Diva Smoothie

- 1 cup Red Endive

- 1 cup chopped Papaya

- 1 banana

- 1 tbsp. chopped fresh Ginger

- 1 cup crushed ice

- 1 tbsp. Cashew butter

- Top with Goji berries

Tomato Onion Smoothie

- 2 Tomatoes

- 1/2 Cucumber

- ¼ cup Cilantro

- 1/2 of small onion

- 1 tbsp. Olive oil

- 1 cup crushed ice

- Juice of 1/2 lime

- 1 Avocado

- Pinch of sea salt

- 1 tbsp. Fresh Basil

Pomegranates & Berries smoothie

- 1 cup Cherries

- ½ cup Raspberries

- 1 cup Pomegranates

- ½ cup Strawberries

- 1 cup Yerba Mate tea

- 1 tbsp. Chlorella

Swiss Peach Smoothie

- 1 cup Red Swiss chard

- ½ cup raspberries, frozen

- 1/2 cup peaches, frozen

- 1 blood orange

- 1 cup crushed ice

- 1 tbsp. Maca

- 1 tbsp. Coconut flakes on top

Avocado Carrot Smoothie

- 2 carrots

- 1 banana

- ½ avocado

- 2 apple

- Juice of ½ lemon

- 1 cup crushed ice

- 1 tsp. ginger

- Top with ½ tsp. Bee Pollen

Radicchio Cranberry Smoothie

- 1 cup fresh Cranberries

- 1 apple

- ½ cup Red Spinach

- ½ Avocado

- 1/2 cup chopped Radicchio

- 1 tbsp. Acai

- 1 cup crushed ice

Red Currants Pumpkin Smoothie

- 1 cup pumpkin puree

- 1 cup red currants

- 1 cup ginger tea

- 1/2 tsp. Lucuma powder

- 1 clove

- Pinch of nutmeg

- Pinch of cinnamon

- 1 tbsp. Chia Seeds

Cucumber Beet Smoothie

- 1 Large Beet

- ½ Cucumber

- 1 Apple

- 1 clove garlic

- 1 tbsp. Minced ginger

- 1 cup crushed ice

- 1 tbsp. Crushed Seaweed (Wakame or Arame)

Rhubarb Avocado Smoothie

- 1 cup chopped Rhubarb

- 1/2 Avocado

- 1 cup hibiscus tea

- 1 tbsp. Cacao nibs

- 1 tbsp. Chopped pecans

- 2 tbsp. Sesame seeds sprinkled

Blood Orange Smoothie

- 2 Blood Oranges

- 2 carrots

- 1 cup Raspberries

- 1 cup hibiscus tea

- 1 tbsp. Walnuts

- 2 tbsp. Ground flax seeds

Papaya Red Spinach Smoothie

- 1 cup chopped Papaya

- 1 banana

- 1 cup red spinach

- 1 cup crushed ice

- 1 tablespoon Maca

- Top with 1 tablespoon dried chokecherries

Red Grapefruit Smoothie

- 1 large red Grapefruit

- 1 cup Red Endive

- 1 cup crushed ice

- 2 tbsp. Sunflower seeds butter

- 1 tbsp. Hemp seeds sprinkled

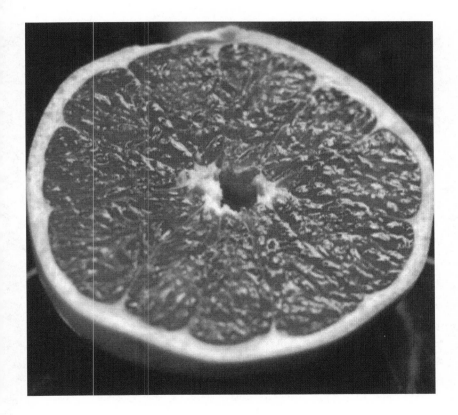

Raspberry Red Lettuce Smoothie

- 1 cup Red Leaf Lettuce

- 1 cup frozen Raspberries

- 2 Red Apples

- 1 tbsp. Goji berries

- 1 cup white tea

Cranberry Red Leaf Lettuce Smoothie

- 1 cups Red Leaf Lettuce
- 1 Banana
- 1 tbsp. Tahini
- 1 cup fresh Cranberries
- 1 cup crushed ice
- Top with Coconut flakes

Frozen Berries Smoothie

1 cup frozen raspberries

1 cup frozen blueberries

1 cup of kefir

Pinch of nutmeg

1 tbsp. Minced ginger

Carrot Pumpkin Parsley Smoothie

2 Carrots

2 cups of chopped pumpkin

1 cup of crushed ice

Pinch of nutmeg

½ tsp. Cinnamon

1 tbsp. Minced parsley

1 tsp. pumpkin seeds

Raspberry Cauliflower Smoothie

2 Cups raspberries

1 cup cauliflower florets

1 cup of crushed ice

1 tsp. Acai

½ tsp. Maqui

1 tbsp. ground flax seeds

Pomegranate Yogurt Smoothie

1 cup Pomegranate seeds

2 ice cubes

1 cup of low fat yogurt

½ tsp. Bee Pollen

1 tbsp. sunflower seeds

Apple Papaya Mint Smoothie

1 chopped Apple

1 chopped Papaya

1 cup of crushed ice

Pinch of nutmeg

½ tsp. Mint

1 tbsp. Papaya Seeds

PURPLE SMOOTHIES

Red Dragon Fruit (Pitaya) Smoothie

- 2 purple carrots
- 2 tbsp. Almond Butter
- 1 cup Red Dragon fruit (Pitaya)
- 1 tbsp. Maca
- 1 Blood Orange
- 1 cup crushed ice

Blueberry Yogurt & Spinach Smoothie

- 1 cup blueberries

- 1 avocado

- 1 cup Red Chard

- 1 cup Yogurt

- 1/2 cup Mulberry

- 1 tbsp. Ground flax seeds

- ½ tsp. Cinnamon

- Top with Blueberries and Coconut flakes

Beet Apple Smoothie

- 1 cup crushed ice

- 1/2 avocado, pitted

- 1 cup frozen strawberries

- 1 lemon, juiced

- 2 chopped celery stalks

- 1 large beet

- 1 apple

- 1 tablespoon coconut oil

- 1 tbsp. Acai

Blueberry Avocado Smoothie

- 1/2 avocado

- 1 cup spinach

- 1 cup blueberries, frozen

- 1 tsp. coconut oil

- 3/4 cup water

- 1 cup crushed ice

- Top with Cranberries

Beet & Beet Smoothie

- 2 cups Beet Greens

- 1 cup crushed ice

- 2 blood oranges,

- 1 large Beet root

- Juice of ½ lemon

- 1 tbsp. Hemp seeds

Chokecherry Cauliflower Smoothie

- 1 cup Chokecherries or 1/2 cup of dried Chokecherries
- ½ cup cauliflower
- 1 cup kefir
- 3 ice cubes
- 1 tbsp. Matcha

Purple Beet Smoothie

- 2 large beets
- ½ Avocado
- 1 cup Raspberry
- 1 tbsp. Chia seeds
- 1 carrot
- 1 cup crushed ice

Purple Cabbage smoothie

- 1 cup Red Cabbage

- ½ Avocado

- 1 Kiwi

- 1 Banana

- 1 Brazil Nut

- 1 cup hibiscus tea

- 1 tbsp. Spirulina

- 1 cup crushed ice

Purple Cauliflower Smoothie

- 1 cup Purple cauliflower

- 1 banana

- 1 cup Black Currants

- 1 tbsp. Chlorella

- 1 cup Chai tea

Acai Strawberries Smoothie

- 1 cup Acai berries or 1/4 cup of Acai powder
- ½ cup strawberries
- 1 cup low-fat plain yogurt
- 3 ice cubes
- 1/2 tsp. Bee Pollen

Red Grapefruit & Beets Smoothie

- 1 Red Grapefruit

- 1 large beet

- 1/2 cup frozen sliced peaches

- 1/2 cup frozen strawberries

- 1 tbsp. Maca

- 1 cup crushed ice

Purple Carrots Smoothie

• 3 purple carrots

• 2 tbsp. Almond Butter

• 1 cup Blackberries

• 1 tbsp. Chlorella

• 1 Orange

• 1 cup crushed ice

Blueberry Banana Smoothie

- 1 cup Blueberries

- 1 apple

- 1 banana

- 1 cup Red endive

- ½ cup crushed ice

- ½ cup water

- Top with Goji berries and shredded coconut

Beet Kale Smoothie

- 1 large beet
- 1 apple
- 1 blood orange
- ½ cup frozen blackberries
- 1 cup kale
- ½ cup crushed ice
- ½ cup water
- 1 tbsp. Hemp Seeds

Purple Kale Smoothie

- 1 cup Purple Kale

- 2 apples

- Ginger

- 1 Banana

- 1 cup frozen Blueberries

- 2 tbsp. Spirulina

- 1 cup Green tea

Purple Queen Smoothie

- 2 purple carrots

- 2 tbsp. Almond Butter

- 1 cup Red Dragon fruit (Pitaya)

- 1 tbsp. Maca

- 1 blood Orange

- 1 cup crushed ice

Black Smoothie

- 2 cups spinach
- 1 cup low fat plain yogurt
- 1 banana
- 1/2 cup blueberries, frozen
- 1 cup blackberries, frozen
- 1 tbsp. Cashew nuts
- 1 cup crushed ice

Blueberry Kefir & Spinach Smoothie

- 1 cup blueberries

- 1 cup chopped Cantaloupe

- 1 cup Red Spinach

- 1 cup Kefir

- 1 tbsp. Hemp seeds

- ½ tsp. Cinnamon

Quatro Lamponi Mirtillo Negress Ribes Smoothie (4 Berries Smoothie)

½ cup raspberries

½ cup blueberries

½ cup blackberries

½ cup red currants

1 cup of crushed ice

Berries Kefir Smoothie

1/2 cup blackberries

½ cup raspberries

1/2 cup of crushed ice

1 cup Kefir

1 tbsp. Chia seeds

Red Currants Blueberry Smoothie

1 cup Red Spinach

1/2 cup blueberries

1/2 cup red currants

1 cup of crushed ice

Pinch of nutmeg

½ tsp. sesame seeds

Blackberry, Buttermilk & Mint Smoothie

- 1 cup blackberries

- 1 avocado

- 1 cup Buttermilk

- 1 tbsp. Ground flax seeds

- a pinch of nutmeg

- Top with mint leaves

Blueberry Buttermilk & Avocado Smoothie

- 1 cup blueberries
- 1 avocado
- 1 cup Buttermilk
- 1 tbsp. Ground flax seeds
- ½ tsp. Cinnamon

GREEN SMOOTHIES

Kale Kiwi Smoothie

- 1 cup Kale, chopped

- 2 Apples

- 2 Kiwis

- 1 tablespoon flax seed

- 1/2 tsp. royal jelly

- 1 cup crushed ice

Zucchini Apples Smoothie

- 1/2 cup zucchini
- 2 Apples
- 3/4 avocado
- 1 stalk Celery
- 1 Lemon
- 1 tbsp. Spirulina
- 1 1/2 cups crushed ice

Dandelion Smoothie

- 1 cup Dandelion greens

- 1 cup Spinach

- ½ cup tahini

- 1 Red Radish

- 1 tbsp. Chia seeds

- 1 cup lavender tea

Broccoli Apple Smoothie

- 1 Apple
- 1 cup Broccoli
- 1 tbsp. Cilantro
- 1 Celery stalk
- 1 cup crushed ice
- 1 tbsp. crushed Seaweed

Salad Smoothie

- 1 cup spinach

- ½ cucumber

- 1/2 small onion

- 2 tablespoons Parsley

- 2 tablespoons lemon juice

- 1 cup crushed ice

- 1 tbsp. olive oil

- ¼ cup Wheatgrass

Avocado Kale Smoothie

- 1 cup Kale

- ½ Avocado

- 1 cup Cucumber

- 1 Celery Stalk

- 1 tbsp. Chia seeds

- 1 cup chamomile tea

- 1 tbsp. Spirulina

Watercress Smoothie

- 1 cup Watercress

- ½ cup almond butter

- 2 small cucumbers

- 1 cup coconut milk

- 1 tbsp. Chlorella

- 1 tbsp. Black cumin– sprinkle on top and garnish with parsley

Beet Greens Smoothie

- 1 cup Beet Greens

- 2 tbsp. Pumpkin seeds butter

- 1 cup Strawberry

- 1 tbsp. Sesame seeds

- 1 tbsp. Hemp seeds

- 1 cup chamomile tea

Broccoli Leeks Cucumber smoothie

- 1 cup Broccoli

- 2 tbsp. Cashew butter

- 2 Leeks

- 2 Cucumbers

- 1 Lime

- ½ cup Lettuce

- ½ cup Leaf Lettuce

- 1 tbsp. Matcha

- 1 cup crushed ice

Cacao Spinach Smoothie

- 2 cups spinach

- 1 cup blueberries, frozen

- 1 tablespoons dark cocoa powder

- ½ cup unsweetened almond milk

- 1/2 cup crushed ice

- 1/2 tsp Lucuma powder

- 1 tbsp. Matcha powder

Flax Almond Butter Smoothie

- ½ cup plain yogurt

- 2 tablespoons almond butter

- 2 cups spinach

- 1 banana, frozen

- 3 strawberries

- 1/2 cup crushed ice

- 1 teaspoon flax seed

Apple Kale Smoothie

- 1 cup kale

- ½ cup coconut milk

- 1 tbsp. Maca

- 1 banana, frozen

- ¼ teaspoon cinnamon

- 1 Apple

- Pinch of nutmeg

- 1 clove

- 3 ice cubes

Iceberg Peach Smoothie

- 1 cup Iceberg lettuce

- 1 Banana

- 1 small peach

- 1 Brazil Nut

- 1 small Mango

- 1 cup Kombucha

- Top with Hemp seeds

Kiwi Apple & Leaf Lettuce Smoothie

- 1 cup Leaf Lettuce

- 2 Apples

- 2 kiwis

- 1/4 Lemon

- 1 tbsp. Chlorella

- 1 cup crushed ice

Banana Spinach Raspberry Smoothie

- 1 cup Spinach

- 2 Bananas

- 2 dates

- ½ cup Raspberries

- 1 tbsp. Ground flax seeds

- 1 cup crushed ice

- 1 tbsp. Cilantro

Endive Apples Smoothie

- 1 cup Endive

- 2 Apples

- 1 Tbsp. Dill

- 1 stalk Celery

- 1/2 Lemon

- 1 tbsp. Matcha

- 1 cup crushed ice

Spinach Celery Parsley Smoothie

- 1 cup Spinach

- 1 Peach

- 1 avocado

- 2 stalks Celery

- 1 Lime

- 1 tbsp. Chia seeds

- 1 cup crushed ice

- 1 tbsp. Parsley

Swiss chard Cucumber Celery Carrot Smoothie

- 1 cup Swiss chard

- 2 Carrots

- 1 Cucumber

- 2 stalks Celery

- 1 Tbsp. Lucuma powder

- 1 tbsp. Parsley

- 1 cup crushed ice

Kale Cucumber Lime Apples Smoothie

- 1 cup Kale
- 2 Apples
- 1 avocado
- 1 Lime
- 1/4 cup Raspberries
- 1 Cucumber
- 1 cup crushed ice

Kiwi Zucchini Smoothie

- 1 cup zucchini

- 2 Apples

- 1/2 avocado

- 2 kiwis

- 1 tbsp. Spirulina

- 1 cup crushed ice

Avocado Kale Smoothie

- 1 cup Kale

- 1 Apple

- 2 avocados

- 1 stalk Celery

- 1/2 Lime

- 1 tbsp. Cilantro

- 1 cup crushed ice

Flax Kiwi Spinach Smoothie

- 1 cup Spinach

- 1 Apple

- 1 banana

- 1 stalk Celery

- 2 Kiwis

- 3 tbsp. ground flax seeds

- 1 cup crushed ice

Parsley Arugula Cucumber Apples Smoothie

- 1 cup Arugula
- 1 Cucumber
- 2 apples
- 1 stalk Celery
- 1 tbsp. Parsley
- 1 cup crushed ice

Celery Cucumber Cabbage Apples Smoothie

- 1/2 cup shredded cabbage

- 1 Apple

- 1 avocado

- 2 stalks Celery

- 1 Lemon

- 1 Zucchini

- 1 cup crushed ice

Kale Banana Apples Smoothie

- 1 cup Kale

- 2 Apples

- 3/4 avocado

- 1 banana

- 1 tbsp. Maqui

- 1 cup crushed ice

Zucchini Celery Apples Smoothie

- 1 zucchini

- 2 Apples

- 3/4 avocado

- 2 stalk Celery

- 1 jalapeno pepper

- 1 cup crushed ice

Leaf Lettuce Apples Spinach Smoothie

- 1/2 cup Spinach

- 2 Apples

- 2 Tbsp. almond butter

- 1 cup Leaf Lettuce

- 1/2 Lemon

- 1 tbsp. Chlorella

- 1 cup crushed ice

Zucchini Parsley Smoothie

- 1 zucchini
- 2 Apples
- ½ cup Parsley
- 1 stalk Celery
- ½ Lime
- 1 tbsp. Sesame seeds
- 1 cup crushed ice

Dandelion Banana Smoothie

- 1 cup Dandelion leaves
- 2 Bananas
- 3/4 avocado
- 1 Orange
- 1 tbsp. Spirulina
- 1 cup crushed ice

Leaf Lettuce Parsley Smoothie

- 1/2 cup Parsley

- 2 Apples

- 1 cup Leaf Lettuce

- 2 Tbsp. Sunflower butter

- 1 Yellow Grapefruit

- 1 tbsp. Hemp Hearts

- 1 cup crushed ice

Chia Apples Spinach Smoothie

- 1 cup Spinach or mustard greens

- 2 Apples

- 2 tbsp. Tahini

- 3 tbsp. Chia seeds

- 1 cup crushed ice

Grapefruit Kale Watercress Smoothie

- 1 large grapefruit

- 1 Apple

- 1 cup watercress

- 2 Kale leaves

- 1 Tbsp. dill (optional)

- 1 cup crushed ice

Collard Greens Parsley and Banana Smoothie

- 1 cup chopped collard greens

- 2 bananas

- 1 Tbsp. chopped parsley

- 1 tbsp. Chlorella

- 1 cup crushed ice

Dandelion Apples Smoothie

- 1 cup Dandelion leaves

- 1 orange

- 3/4 avocado

- 1 stalk Celery or 1 broccoli floret

- 1 tsp. chopped fresh ginger

- 1 cup crushed ice

Swiss Chard & Orange Smoothie

- 1 cup Swiss chard leaves

- 1 orange

- 3/4 avocado

- 1 cup crushed ice

Chia, Spinach & Kiwi Smoothie

- 1 cup Spinach leaves
- 3 kiwis
- 1 Tbsp. tahini
- 1 3 Tbsp. Chia seeds
- 1 cup crushed ice

Apple Kiwi Smoothie

- 2 Apples, cored, cubed

- 2 kiwis

- 3/4 avocado

- 1 stalk Celery or 1 broccoli floret

- 1 cup crushed ice

Endive & Banana Smoothie

- 1 cup Endive leaves

- 1 banana

- 3/4 almond butter

- 1 broccoli floret

- 1 cup crushed ice

Iceberg Lettuce & Grapefruit Smoothie

- 1 cup Iceberg Lettuce leaves

- 1 large Grapefruit

- 3/4 avocado

- 1 cauliflower floret

- 1 tbsp. Lucuma powder

- 1 cup crushed ice

Pear, Parsley, Cilantro & Lemon Smoothie

- 1 cup Parsley leaves

- 1 pear

- 3/4 avocado

- ½ lemon - juice

- 1 tbsp. chopped Cilantro

- 1 cup crushed ice

Kale Grapefruit Smoothie

- 1 cup Dandelion leaves

- 1 grapefruit

- 3/4 avocado

- 1 tbsp. Lucuma powder

- 1 cup crushed ice

Dandelion Banana Smoothie

- 1 cup Dandelion leaves
- 1 banana
- 3/4 avocado
- 1 tbsp. Lucuma powder
- 1 cup crushed ice

Yellow Pumpkin, Peach & Spinach Smoothie

- 1 cup Spinach leaves
- 1 cup cooked yellow pumpkin
- 1 cup cubed peach
- 3/4 avocado
- a pinch of nutmeg and cinnamon
- 1 tbsp. lucuma
- 1 cup crushed ice

Papaya, Peach & Spinach Smoothie

- 1 cup Spinach leaves
- 1 cup cubed papaya
- 3/4 avocado
- 1 cup cubed peach
- 1 cup crushed ice

Arugula Celery Apples Smoothie

- 1 cup Arugula or spinach
- 2 Apples
- 2 Tbsp. almond butter
- 1 tbsp. Chia seeds
- 1 cup crushed ice

Barley Grass Smoothie

- 1 cup barley grass or any other leafy greens

- 2 bananas

- 1 tbsp. chopped cilantro

- 1/4 lime

- 1 tsp. Spirulina

- 1 cup crushed ice

Chamomile Banana & Swiss Chard Smoothie

- 1/2 cup Swiss chard

- 2 bananas

- 3/4 avocado

- 1 tsp. edible chamomile for decoration

- 1 tbsp. Spirulina

- 1 cup chamomile tea

Granny Smith & Celery Smoothie

- 1 cup chopped celery

- 2 Granny Smith Apples

- 3/4 avocado

- 1 Lime

- 1 tbsp. Spirulina

- 1 1/2 cups crushed ice

WHITE SMOOTHIES

White Cauliflower Smoothie

• 1 cup Kefir

• 1 cup White cauliflower florets

• 1 fig

• Juice of ½ lemon

• 1/2 cup crushed ice

• 1 tbsp. Minced ginger

• 1 tbsp. Maca

• few Hazelnuts

Coconut Chia Pudding

- 1/4 cup Chia seeds

- 1 cup coconut milk

- 1/2 tablespoon Royall jelly

- 1 tsp. Ground Vanilla Bean

- a pinch of Nutmeg

- Top with Blueberries

White Kefir Smoothie

- ½ cup plain kefir

- 1 banana

- 1 tablespoon sunflower butter

- 1 tbsp. Maca

- ½ tsp. Cinnamon

- Top with Apple slices, cherries and lime

Tzataziki Smoothie

- 1 cup kefir or plain Greek yogurt
- 1 cucumber
- 1 avocado
- 1 tbsp. Fresh dill or mint
- 1 tablespoon lemon juice
- 1 teaspoon sea salt
- 1 teaspoon Sesame seeds

Coconut Smoothie

- 1 cup of Coconut Milk

- 1 banana

- 1 White Peach

- 1 tablespoon tahini

- 1 tbsp. Hemp seeds

- a pinch of Nutmeg

- Top with Coconut flakes

Cacao Blackberries Chia Pudding

- 1/4 cup Chia seeds

- 1 cup coconut milk

- 1/2 tsp. Lucuma

- 1 tbsp. Maca

- Top with Blackberries

Coconut Yogurt Smoothie

- 1 Cup of low fat Greek Yogurt

- 1 banana

- 1 tablespoon Coconut flakes

- 1 tablespoon Hemp seeds

- Top with whipped Coconut Cream

Coconut Pomegranate Chia Pudding

- 1/4 cup Chia seeds

- 1 cup Coconut milk

- 1/2 tsp Lucuma powder

- 1/2 tablespoon Coconut flakes

- Top with Pomegranate seeds

Yellow Smoothies

Cauliflower Smoothie

- 1 cup White cauliflower florets

- 1 small Mango

- 1 passion fruit

- 1/2 tsp. Bee Pollen

- 1 cup crushed ice

- Pinch of nutmeg

Papaya Smoothie

- 1 banana

- 1 cup spinach

- 1 cup chopped papaya

- 1 cup crushed ice

- 1 tbsp. Chia seeds

Swiss Papaya Smoothie

- 1 Papaya
- 1 Banana
- 1 cup Swiss chard
- 1 cup Lemongrass tea
- 1 tbsp. Matcha

Pumpkin Banana Smoothie

- 1 cup pumpkin puree

- 1 banana

- 1 cup ginger tea

- 1/2 tsp. Lucuma powder

- 1 clove

- Pinch of nutmeg

- Pinch of cinnamon

- Top with Hemp seeds

Rainbow Smoothie

3 Colors Rainbow Smoothie

- Blend 1 Large beet with some crushed ice

- Blend 3 carrots with some crashed ice

- Blend 1 cucumber, 1 cup of leaf lettuce, some ice and ½ cup Wheatgrass

- Serve them separate to preserve the distinct color

Blackberry & Strawberries Smoothie

- 1 cup Blackberries

- 1 cup Strawberries

- 1/2 cup Blueberries

- 1 cup crushed ice

Blueberry Blackberry Smoothie

- 1 cup Blueberries

- 1 cup Blackberries

- 1 Avocado

- 1 cup crushed ice

Strawberry Coconut Milk Smoothie

- 2 cups Strawberries

- 1 cup coconut milk

Raspberry Grapefruit Smoothie

- 1 cup Raspberries

- 2 Grapefruits

- 1 tbsp. ground coconut flakes

- 1 cup crushed ice

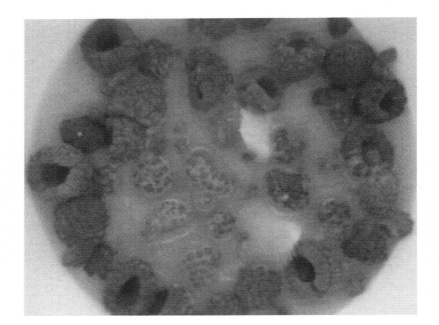

Goji Blueberries Smoothie

- 1/2 cup dried Goji berries

- 1 cup Raspberries

- 1 cup Blueberries

- 1 cup coconut milk

Avocado Mango Smoothie

- 1 cup Raspberries

- 1 cup Strawberries

- 1/2 cup Blueberries

- 1 cup kefir

Orange Blueberry Smoothie

- 1 Orange

- 1cup Blueberries

- 1 Grapefruit

- 1 cup crushed ice

Carrot Apricot Smoothie

- 1 Orange

- 3 carrots

- 4 apricots

- 1 cup crushed ice

Banana Blueberry Mulberry Acai Smoothie

- 1 Banana

- 1cup Blueberries

- 1 cup Mulberry

- 1 cup crushed ice

- 1 tbsp. acai powder

Kiwi Banana Grape Smoothie

- 1 banana

- 1cup seedless grapes

- 1 cup Strawberries

- 1 cup crushed ice

- 1 sliced kiwi

- 1 sliced mango (optionally - use an apple)

Carrot Raspberry Smoothie

- 1 banana

- 1cup Raspberries

- 3 Carrots

- 1 cup crushed ice

Boysenberry Peach Smoothie

- 1 Peach (optionally - use an apple)

- 1 cup Boysenberries

- 1 cup yogurt

Mango Raspberry Smoothie

- 1 mango cut in cubes (optionally - use an apple)
- 1cup frozen raspberries
- 2 Tbsp. pecans
- 1 cup crushed ice

Peach Carrot Smoothie

- 2 Peaches (optionally - use an apple)

- 1 banana

- 3 carrots

- 1 cup crushed ice

Raspberry Mango Chia Smoothie

- 2 cups Raspberries

- 1 mango, cubed

- 1 Tbsp. chia seeds

- 1 Tbsp. hemp seeds

- 1 cup crushed ice

Apricot Carrot Smoothie

- 5 Apricots

- 1 banana

- 3 carrots

- 1 cup crushed ice

Pumpkin Carrot Smoothie

- 2 cups pumpkin, cubed

- 1 banana

- 2 carrots

- 1 cup crushed ice

Red Grapefruit Banana Smoothie

- 1 red grapefruit

- 2 bananas

- 1 cup crushed ice

Pumpkin Peach Smoothie

- 2 Peaches

- 1 cup pumpkin

- 1 banana

- 1 cup crushed ice

Orange Cucumber Smoothie

- 1 Orange
- 1 banana
- 1 cucumber
- 1/4 cup blueberries
- 1/4 Yogurt & 1 Tsp. honey
- 1 cup crushed ice

Banana Blueberry Blackberry Smoothie

- 1 cup blueberries

- 1 banana

- 1 cup blackberries

- 1 cup crushed ice

Blackberry Banana Smoothie

- 1 cup Blackberries

- 1 banana

- 1/4 Kefir & 1 tsp. Honey

- 1 cup crushed ice

Kefir Blueberry Mixed Greens Smoothie

- 1 cup Kefir

- 1 cup blueberries

- 1 cup mixed greens

- 1 cup crushed ice

Banana Orange Mixed Greens Smoothie

- 1 Orange
- 1 banana
- 1 cup mixed greens
- 1/2 cup blackberries
- 1 cup crushed ice

Celery Kale Avocado Smoothie

- 1 cup celery
- 1 avocado
- 1 cup kale
- 1 cup crushed ice

Cucumber Watermelon Strawberries Spinach Smoothie

- 1 Cucumber
- 1 cup watermelon
- 1 cup Spinach
- 1 cup strawberries
- 1 cup crushed ice

Kale Blueberries Blackberries Grapefruit Smoothie

- 1 Grapefruit

- 1 cup blackberries

- 1 cup mixed greens

- 1/2 cup blueberries

- 1 cup crushed ice

Kefir Kale Banana Orange Chia Smoothie

- 1/2 Orange

- 1 banana

- 1 cup Kale

- 1/4 cup chia seeds

- 1/2 cup kefir

- 1 cup crushed ice

Spinach Almond Milk Banana Apple Smoothie

- 1 cup Almond milk

- 1 banana

- 1 cup spinach

- 1 apple

- 1/2 cup crushed ice

Spinach Apple Banana Avocado Celery Smoothie

- 1 Apple
- 1 banana
- 1 cup Spinach
- 1/2 avocado
- 1 cup Celery
- 1 cup crushed ice

Spinach Banana Strawberries Grapefruit Flax Seeds Smoothie

- 1 cup Strawberries

- 1 banana

- 1 cup Spinach

- 1/2 Grapefruit

- 2 Tbsp. Flax seeds

- 1 cup crushed ice

Spinach Blackberry Blueberry Smoothie

- 1 cup frozen blueberries

- 1 cup frozen blackberries

- 1 cup spinach

- 1 cup crushed ice

Spinach Kale Apple Orange Avocado Lemon Smoothie

- 1 Apple
- 1 orange or 2 small ones
- 1/2 cup Spinach
- 1/2 cup Kale
- 1/2 avocado
- 1/2 lemon
- 1 cup crushed ice

Strawberries Watermelon Spinach Celery Smoothie

- 1 cup refrigerated Strawberries

- 1 celery stalk

- 1 cup spinach

- 1 cup refrigerated watermelon

- 1/2 cup crushed ice

Kale Banana Red Grapefruit Smoothie

- 1 banana
- 1 large red grapefruit
- 1 Tsp. minced ginger
- 1 cup Kale
- 1 cup crushed ice

Kale Strawberries Avocado Smoothie

- 1 cup Strawberries

- 1 cup Kale

- 1/2 avocado

- 1/2 lemon

- 1 cup crushed ice

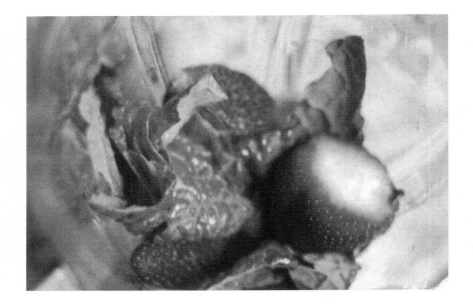

Peach Carrot Avocado Lemon Smoothie

- 1 peach
- 1 cup sliced carrots
- 1/2 avocado
- 1/2 lemon
- 1 cup crushed ice

Blueberries Spinach Banana Strawberries Blueberries Smoothie

- 1 banana

- 1 cup spinach

- 1/2 cup frozen blueberries

- 1/2 cup frozen strawberries

- 1/2 cup frozen blackberries

- 1 cup crushed ice

Celery Peach Banana Carrot Lemon Smoothie

- 2 stalks celery

- 1 cup sliced carrot or 4 baby carrots

- 1 banana

- 1 peach

- 1/2 lemon

- 1 cup crushed ice

Pollen Banana Spinach Blackberries Smoothie

- 1 banana

- 1 cup spinach

- 1 cup frozen blackberries

- 1 Tsp. pollen

- 1 cup crushed ice

Apple Ginger Tomato Celery Kale Parsley Avocado Smoothie

- 1 Apple

- 1 medium size tomato

- 1/4 cup parsley

- 1/2 cup Kale

- 1 tsp. minced ginger

- 1 celery stalk

- 1/2 avocado

- 1/2 lemon

- 1 cup crushed ice

Layered Raspberry Kale Avocado Lemon Banana Smoothie

- 1 cup raspberry – blended and set aside

- 1 banana

- 1/2 cup Kale

- 1/2 avocado

- 1/2 lemon

- 1 cup crushed ice

Mix all ingredients except raspberry and then pour half of it in a jar or a glass. Then pour blended raspberry over and then pour the second half of the kale smoothie over.

Goji Kiwi Banana Orange Smoothie

- 2 Kiwis

- 1 orange or 2 small ones

- 1 banana

- 1/2 cup dry goji berries

- 1 cup crushed ice

Almond Milk Raspberry Blueberry Smoothie

- 1 cup almond milk
- 1 cup frozen raspberries
- 1 cup frozen blueberries
- 1 cup crushed ice

Mellon Kiwi Watermelon Smoothie

- 3 kiwis

- 2 cups cubed watermelon

- 1/2 cup melon

- 1/2 cup spinach (to slow down sugar absorption)

- 1 mint leaf

- 1 cup crushed ice

Melon Seedless Green Grapes Mint Smoothie

- 1 cup seedless green grapes

- 1 cup cubed melon

- 1 cup spinach (to slow down sugar absorption)

- 1 mint leaf

- 1 cup crushed ice

Kiwi Chamomile Banana Pollen Smoothie

- 1 banana
- 3 kiwis
- 1/2 cup spinach
- 1 Tsp. dried chamomile
- 1 cup crushed ice or cold chamomile tea

Blueberry Chamomile Banana Blackberry Strawberry Smoothie

- 1 banana
- 1/2 cup strawberries
- 1/2 cup frozen blueberries
- 1 Tsp. dried chamomile
- 1/2 cup spinach
- 1 cup crushed ice or cold chamomile tea

Oats Banana Blueberry Strawberry Smoothie

- 1 banana
- 1 cup oats soaked in almond milk overnight
- 1/2 cup frozen blueberries
- 1/2 cup raspberries
- 3 mint leaves
- 1/2 cup crushed ice

Mango Banana Hemp Seeds Smoothie

- 1 banana

- 1/2 mango, cubed

- 1 Tsp. hemp seeds

- 1/2 cup spinach

- 1 cup crushed ice or cold chamomile tea

Raspberries Banana Blackberries Strawberries Smoothie

- 1 banana

- 1/2 cup spinach

- 1/2 cup frozen blackberries

- 1/2 cup frozen raspberries

- 1/2 cup strawberries

- 1 Tsp. pollen

- 1 cup crushed ice

Oats Kefir Orange Banana Chia Smoothie

- 1 banana

- 1 cup oats soaked in kefir for at least 30 minutes

- 1 orange

- 1/2 cup crushed ice

- 1 Tsp. chia seeds, soaked with oats in kefir at the same time

Kale Avocado Spinach Orange Apple Smoothie

- 1 small orange

- 1/2 cup spinach

- 1/2 cup Kale

- 1/2 half apple

- 1 avocado

- 1 cup crushed ice

Kefir Strawberries Green Tea Blueberries Smoothie

- ½ cup kefir
- 1 cup cold green tea
- 1 cup frozen blueberries
- 1 cup strawberries
- 1 Tsp. pollen
- 1/2 cup crushed ice

Almond Milk Avocado Almonds Kale Smoothie

- 1 banana
- 1 cup almond milk
- 1 cup kale
- 1/2 avocado
- 1/2 cup crushed ice
- 1 Tbsp. slivered almonds

Apples Pears Cinnamon Hemp Seeds Smoothie

- 1 pear

- 1 cup oats soaked in kefir for at least 30 minutes

- 2 apples

- 1 cup crushed ice

- 1 Tbsp. hemp seeds

- 1 Tsp. cinnamon

Apple Banana Kiwi Spinach Smoothie

- 1 banana
- 1 pear
- 1 kiwi
- 1 cup spinach
- 1 cup crushed ice

Apple Spinach Yogurt Flax Smoothie

- 1 apple

- 1 cup spinach

- 1 cup yogurt

- 1/2 cup crushed ice

- 1 Tbsp. ground flax seeds

Banana Peach Apricot Ginger Smoothie

- 1 banana
- 1 peach
- 1 apricot
- 1 cup crushed ice
- 1 Tsp. minced ginger

Beet Leaf Mint Celery Banana Chia Radish Smoothie

- 1 banana

- 1 cup celery

- 3 mint leaves

- 1 cup beet leaves

- ¼ cup radish

- 1 cup crushed ice

- 1 Tsp. chia seeds

Cinnamon Banana Coconut Milk Apple Ginger Turmeric Smoothie

- 1 banana

- 1 cup coconut milk

- 1 apple

- ½ tsp. cinnamon

- 1 tsp. minced ginger

- 1/2 cup crushed ice

- 1/4 Tsp. turmeric

Ginger Grapefruit Banana Carrot Smoothie

- 1 banana

- 2 carrots

- 1 red grapefruit

- 1 cup crushed ice

- 1 Tsp. minced ginger

Kale Parsley Apricot Apple Smoothie

- 1 banana
- 1 apple
- 1 apricot
- 1 cup kale
- ¼ cup parsley
- 1 cup crushed ice

Kale Parsley Celery Oats Flax Smoothie

- 1 banana

- 1 cup kale

- 1/4 cup parsley

- 1 cup celery

- 1/4 cup oats

- 1 cup crushed ice

- 1 Tsp. ground flax seeds

Beet Kiwi Grapefruit Smoothie

- 1 beet
- 1 red grapefruit
- 2 kiwis
- 1 tsp. minced ginger
- 1/2 cup crushed ice

Blackberries Coconut Milk Banana Smoothie

- 1 cup blackberries

- 1 cup coconut milk

- 1 banana

- 1/2 cup crushed ice

Coconut Milk Orange Goji Chia Smoothie

- 1 banana

- 1 cup coconut milk

- 1 orange

- 1 tbsp. chia seeds

- 1/2 cup crushed ice

- 1 Tbsp. goji berries

Coconut Milk Raspberry Banana Smoothie

- 1 banana

- 1 cup coconut milk

- 1 cup raspberries

- 1 tbsp. shredded coconut

- 1/2 cup crushed ice

Ginger Avocado Yogurt Apple Smoothie

- 1 avocado

- 1 cup yogurt

- 1 apple

- ½ tsp. cinnamon

- 1 tsp. minced ginger

- 1/2 cup crushed ice

- 2 Tbsp. parsley

Granny Smith Avocado Coconut Milk Spinach Smoothie

- 1 banana
- 1 cup coconut milk
- 1 granny smith apple
- 1 cup spinach
- 1/2 lemon
- 1/2 cup crushed ice

Granny Smith Blueberries Avocado Smoothie

- 1 avocado

- 1 granny smith apple

- ½ tsp. cinnamon

- 1 cup blueberries

- 1 cup crushed ice

Red Grapefruit Banana Raspberry Spinach Smoothie

- 1 banana

- 1 red grapefruit

- 1 cup raspberries

- 1 cup spinach

- 1 tsp. minced ginger

- 1/2 cup crushed ice

Spinach Pomegranate Banana Kiwi Ginger Smoothie

- 1 banana

- 1 cup coconut milk

- 1 cup spinach

- 1 Tbsp. pomegranate seeds for sprinkling

- 1 tsp. minced ginger

- 1/2 cup crushed ice

- 2 kiwis

Swiss Chard Blackberry Smoothie

- 1 banana

- 1 cup coconut milk

- 1 cup blackberries

- 1 cup Swiss chard

- 1 tsp. minced ginger

- 1/2 cup crushed ice

Superfoods Reference Book

Unfortunately, I had to take out the whole Superfoods Reference Book out of all of my books because parts of that book are featured on my blog. I joined Kindle Direct Publishing Select program which allows me to have all my books free for 5 days every 3 months. Unfortunately, KDP Select program also means that all my books have to have unique content that is not available in any other online store or on the Internet (including my blog). I didn't want to remove parts of Superfoods Reference book that is already on my blog because I want that all people have free access to that information. I also wanted to be part of KDP Select program because that is an option to give my book for free to anyone. So, some sections of my Superfoods Reference Book can be found on my blog, under Superfoods menu on my blog. Complete Reference book is available for subscribers to my Superfoods Today Newsletter. Subscribers to my Newsletter will also get information whenever any of my books becomes free on Amazon. I will not offer any product pitches or anything similar to my subscribers, only Superfoods related information, recipes and weight loss and fitness tips. So, subscribe to my newsletter, download Superfoods Cookbook Book Two free eBook which has complete Superfood Reference book included and have the opportunity to get all of my future books for free.

ORAC Value List

ORAC is short for Oxygen Radical Absorbance Capacity. It was developed by the National Institutes of Health in Baltimore.

ORAC units are measurement of the antioxidant capacity of foods. The higher the ORAC value, the more antioxidants the food has.

Foods high in antioxidants lower the risks of cancer and disease.

You'll notice that spices have the most antioxidants. But the ORAC value is measured in dry spices and that is why the values are so high. Common foods such as berries, beans and apples have much fewer antioxidants per gram, because they are full of water. Plus, you can't eat 6 oz. of cloves in one meal, but you can eat 6 oz. of apples. You will notice that e.g. white raisins have higher ORAC value than grape seeds although they are pretty much the same food, but that is because raisins have less water. Every food on this list above value 2 is great. It's better not to pay too much attention to exact ORAC number, just keep eating them all and try to squeeze as much top rated foods as you can. ORAC values in the table are divided per 1000, e.g. Cloves have ORAC rating over 314000, but I slashed 1000 off of each value to keep it easier to compare. Chia seeds are not on this list, but they have value around 6.

1	Cloves, ground	314
2	Sumac bran	312
3	Cinnamon, ground	268
4	Sorghum, bran, raw	240
5	Oregano, dried	200
6	Turmeric, ground	159
7	Acai berry, freeze-dried	103
8	Sorghum, bran, black	101
9	Sumac, grain, raw	87
10	Cocoa powder, unsweetened	81
11	Cumin seed	77
12	Maqui berry, powder	75
13	Parsley, dried	74
14	Sorghum, bran, red	71
15	Basil, dried	68
16	Baking chocolate, unsweetened	50
17	Curry powder	49
18	Sorghum, grain, hi-tannin	45
19	Chocolate, dutched powder	40
20	Maqui berry, juice	40

21	Sage	32
22	Mustard seed, yellow	29
23	Ginger, ground	29
24	Pepper, black	28
25	Thyme, fresh	27
26	Marjoram, fresh	27
27	Goji berries	25
28	Rice bran, crude	24
29	Chili powder	24
30	Sorghum, grain, black	22
31	Chocolate, dark	21
32	Flax hull lignans	20
33	Chocolate, semisweet	18
34	Pecans	18
35	Paprika	18
36	Chokeberry, raw	16
37	Tarragon, fresh	16
38	Ginger root, raw	15
39	Elderberries, raw	15
40	Sorghum, grain, red	14

41	Peppermint, fresh	14
42	Oregano, fresh	14
43	Walnuts	14
44	Hazelnuts	10
45	Cranberries, raw	10
46	Pears, dried	9
47	Savory, fresh	9
48	Artichokes	9
49	Kidney beans, red	8
50	Pink beans	8
51	Black beans	8
52	Pistachio nuts	8
53	Currants	8
54	Pinto beans	8
55	Plums	8
56	Chocolate, milk chocolate	8
57	Lentils	7
58	Agave, dried	7
59	Apples, dried	7
60	Garlic powder	7

61	Blueberries	7
62	Prunes	7
63	Sorghum, bran, white	6
64	Lemon balm, leaves	6
65	Soybeans	6
66	Onion powder	6
67	Blackberries	5
68	Garlic, raw	5
69	Cilantro leaves	5
70	Wine, Cabernet Sauvignon	5
71	Raspberries	5
72	Basil, fresh	5
73	Almonds	4
74	Dill weed	4
75	Cowpeas	4
76	Apples, red delicious	4
77	Peaches, dried	4
78	Raisins, white	4
79	Apples, granny smith	4
80	Dates	4

81	Wine, red	4
82	Strawberries	4
83	Peanut butter, smooth	3
84	Currants, red	3
85	Figs	3
86	Cherries	3
87	Gooseberries	3
88	Apricots, dried	3
89	Peanuts, all types	3
90	Cabbage, red	3
91	Broccoli	3
92	Apples	3
93	Raisins	3
94	Pears	3
95	Agave	3
96	Blueberry juice	3
97	Cardamom	2,7
98	Guava	2,5
99	Lettuce, red leaf	2,38
100	Concord grape juice	2,37

101	Cereals, ready-to-eat, corn flakes	2,36
102	Juice, Pomegranate, 100%	2,34
103	Cereals, oats, instant, fortified, plain, dry	2,31
104	Cereals ready-to-eat, granola, low-fat, with raisins	2,29
105	Cabbage, red, raw	2,25
106	Apples, Golden Delicious, raw, without skin	2,21
107	Sorghum, grain, white	2,20
108	Radish seeds, sprouted, raw	2,18
109	Cereals ready-to-eat, oat bran	2,18
110	Cereals ready-to-eat, toasted oatmeal	2,18
111	Cereals, oats, quick, uncooked	2,17
112	Asparagus, raw	2,15
113	Cereals ready-to-eat, oatmeal, toasted squares	2,14
114	Sweet potato, cooked, baked in skin, without salt	2,12
115	Bread, butternut whole grain	2,10
116	Chives, raw	2,09
117	Cabbage, savoy, cooked, boiled, drained, without salt	2,05
118	Prune juice, canned	2,04
119	Guava, red-fleshed	1,99
120	Applesauce, canned, unsweetened, without added ascorbic acid	1,97

121	Bread, pumpernickel	1,96
122	Nuts, cashew nuts, raw	1,95
123	Beet greens, raw	1,95
124	Avocados, Hass, raw	1,93
125	Pears, green cultivars, with peel, raw	1,91
126	Rocket, raw	1,90
127	Oranges, raw, navels	1,82
128	Peaches, raw	1,81
129	Juice, red grape	1,79
130	Cabbage, black, cooked	1,77
131	Beets, raw	1,77
132	Pears, red anjou, raw	1,75
133	Snacks, popcorn, air-popped	1,74
134	Radishes, raw	1,74
135	Cereals, oats, old fashioned, uncooked	1,71
136	Tortilla chips, reduced fat, Olestra - TEMPORARY	1,70
137	Nuts, macadamia nuts, dry roasted, without salt added	1,70
138	Spinach, frozen, chopped or leaf, unprepared	1,69
139	Potatoes, Russet, flesh and skin, baked	1,68
140	Asparagus, cooked, boiled, drained	1,64

141	Tangerines, (mandarin oranges), raw	1,62
142	Broccoli raab, cooked	1,55
143	Grapefruit, raw, pink and red, all areas	1,55
144	Onions, red, raw	1,52
145	Beans, navy, mature seeds, raw	1,52
146	Cereals ready-to-eat, QUAKER, QUAKER OAT LIFE, plain	1,52
147	Spinach, raw	1,52
148	Alfalfa seeds, sprouted, raw	1,51
149	Juice, Cranberry/Concord grape	1,48
150	Lettuce, green leaf, raw	1,45
151	Lettuce, butterhead (includes boston and bibb types), raw	1,42
152	Bread, mixed-grain (includes whole-grain, 7-grain)	1,42
153	Nuts, brazilnuts, dried, unblanched	1,42
154	Broccoli, raw	1,36
155	Potatoes, red, flesh and skin, baked	1,33
156	Potatoes, russet, flesh and skin, raw	1,32
157	Bread, Oatnut	1,32
158	Cereals ready-to-eat, wheat, shredded, plain, sugar and salt free	1,30
159	Parsley, raw	1,30
160	Milk, chocolate, fluid, commercial, reduced fat	1,26

161	Grapes, red, raw	1,26
162	Tea, green, brewed	1,25
163	Agave, raw (Southwest)	1,25
164	Grapefruit juice, white, raw	1,24
165	Lemon juice, raw	1,23
166	Onions, yellow, sauteed	1,22
167	Kiwi, gold, raw	1,21
168	Olive oil, extra-virgin	1,15
169	Potatoes, white, flesh and skin, baked	1,14
170	Tea, brewed, prepared with tap water	1,13
171	Grapes, white or green, raw	1,12
172	Apricots, raw	1,12
173	Potatoes, red, flesh and skin, raw	1,10
174	Potatoes, white, flesh and skin, raw	1,06
175	Onions, raw	1,03
176	Alcoholic beverage, wine, table, rose	1,01
177	Mangos, raw	1,00
178	Juice, strawberry	1,00
179	Sauce, ready-to-serve, salsa	1,00
180	Peppers, sweet, orange, raw	0,98

181	Peppers, sweet, yellow, raw	0,97
182	Lettuce, cos or romaine, raw	0,96
183	Soybeans, mature seeds, sprouted, raw	0,96
184	Eggplant, raw	0,93
185	Peppers, sweet, green, raw	0,92
186	Beans, pinto, mature seeds, cooked, boiled, without salt	0,90
187	Sweet potato, raw, unprepared	0,90
188	Pineapple, raw, extra sweet variety	0,88
189	Kiwi fruit, (chinese gooseberries), fresh, raw	0,88
190	Bananas, raw	0,88
191	Juice, cranberrry, 100% - cranberry blend, red	0,87
192	Onions, white, raw	0,86
193	Cabbage, cooked, boiled, drained, without salt	0,86
194	Chickpeas (garbanzo beans, bengal gram), mature seeds, raw	0,85
195	Peppers, sweet, red, sauteed	0,85
196	Raisins, white, fresh (purchased in Italy)	0,83
197	Cauliflower, raw	0,83
198	Lime juice, raw	0,82
199	Grape juice, white	0,79
200	Peppers, sweet, red, raw	0,79

201	Olive oil, extra-virgin, w/parsley, home prepared	0,77
202	Sweet potato, cooked, boiled, without skin	0,77
203	Beans, snap, green, raw	0,76
204	Nectarines, raw	0,75
205	Peas, yellow, mature seeds, raw	0,74
206	Chilchen (Red Berry Beverage) (Navajo)	0,74
207	Corn, sweet, yellow, raw	0,73
208	Orange juice, raw	0,73
209	Pear juice, all varieties	0,70
210	Peppers, sweet, yellow, grilled	0,69
211	Tomato products, canned, sauce	0,69
212	Mush, blue corn with ash (Navajo)	0,68
213	Olive oil, extra-virgin, w/basil, home prepared	0,68
214	Carrots, raw	0,67
215	Cauliflower, cooked, boiled, drained, without salt	0,62
216	Nuts, pine nuts, dried	0,62
217	Peppers, sweet, green, sauteed	0,62
218	Onions, sweet, raw	0,61
219	Peas, green, frozen, unprepared	0,60
220	Catsup	0,58
221	Pineapple juice, canned, unsweetened, without added ascorbic acid	0,57

222	Vinegar, Apple	0,56
223	Pineapple, raw, traditional varieties	0,56
224	Olive oil, extra-virgin, w/garlic, home prepared	0,56
225	Vegetable juice cocktail, canned	0,55
226	Tomatoes, plum, raw	0,55
227	Peas, split, mature seeds, raw	0,52
228	Corn, sweet, yellow, frozen, kernels cut off cob, unprepared	0,52
229	Cabbage, raw	0,51
230	Celery, raw	0,50
231	Broccoli, frozen, spears, unprepared	0,50
232	Leeks, (bulb and lower leaf-portion), raw	0,49
233	Tomato juice, canned, with salt added	0,49
234	Cocoa mix, powder	0,49
235	Pumpkin, raw	0,48
236	Spices, poppy seed	0,48
237	Lettuce, iceberg (includes crisphead types), raw	0,44
238	Carrots, baby, raw	0,44
239	Peaches, canned, heavy syrup, drained	0,44
240	Babyfood, juice, pear	0,41
241	Corn, sweet, yellow, canned, brine pack, regular pack, solids and liquids	0,41

242	Vinegar, Red wine	0,41
243	Apple juice, canned or bottled, unsweetened, without added ascorbic acid	0,41
244	Tomatoes, red, ripe, cooked	0,41
245	Squash, winter, butternut, raw	0,40
246	Alcoholic beverage, wine, table, white	0,39
247	Pineapple, raw, all varieties	0,39
248	Tomatoes, red, ripe, raw, year round average	0,37
249	Carrots, cooked, boiled, drained, without salt	0,32
250	Melons, cantaloupe, raw	0,32
251	Fennel, bulb, raw	0,31
252	Beans, snap, green variety, canned, regular pack, solids and liquids	0,29
253	Vinegar, Apple and Honey	0,27
254	Eggplant, cooked, boiled, drained, without salt	0,25
255	Beans, lima, immature seeds, canned, regular pack, solids and liquids	0,24
256	Melons, honeydew, raw	0,24
257	Juice, cranberry, white	0,23
258	Vinegar, Honey	0,23
259	Olive oil, extra-virgin, w/garlic and red hot peppers, home prepared	0,22
260	Cucumber, with peel, raw	0,21
261	Squash, summer, zucchini, includes skin, raw	0,18
262	Watermelon, raw	0,14
263	Cucumber, peeled, raw	0,13
264	Oil, peanut, salad or cooking	0,11
265	Limes, raw	0,08

Your Free Gift

As a way of saying thanks for your purchase, I'm offering you my FREE eBook that is exclusive to my book and blog readers.

Superfoods Cookbook Book Two has over 70 Superfoods recipes and complements Superfoods Cookbook Book One and it contains Superfoods Salads, Superfoods Smoothies and Superfoods Deserts with ultra-healthy non-refined ingredients. All ingredients are 100% Superfoods.

It also contains Superfoods Reference book which is organized by Superfoods (more than 60 of them, with the list of their benefits), Superfoods spices, all vitamins, minerals and antioxidants. Superfoods Reference Book lists Superfoods that can help with 12 diseases and 9 types of cancer.

Other Books from this Author

Superfoods Today Diet is a Kindle Superfoods Diet that gives you 4 week Superfoods Diet meal plan as well as 2 weeks maintenance meal plan and recipes for weight loss success. It is an extension of Detox book and it's written for people who want to switch to Superfoods lifestyle.

Superfoods Today Body Care is a Kindle with over 50 Natural Recipes for beautiful skin and hair. It has body scrubs, facial masks and hair care recipes made with the best Superfoods like avocado honey, coconut, olive oil, oatmeal, yogurt, banana and Superfoods herbs like lavender, rosemary, mint, sage, hibiscus, rose.

Superfoods Today Cookbook is a Kindle that contains over 160 Superfoods recipes created with 100% Superfoods ingredients. Most of the meals can be prepared in under 30 minutes and some are really quick ones that can be done in 10 minutes only. Each recipe combines Superfoods ingredients that deliver astonishing amounts of antioxidants, essential fatty acids (like omega-3), minerals, vitamins, and more.

Superfoods Today Smoothies is a Kindle Superfoods Smoothies with over 70+ 100% Superfoods smoothies. Featured are Red, Purple, Green and Yellow Smoothies

Superfoods Today Salads is a Kindle that contains over 60 Superfoods Salads recipes created with 100% Superfoods ingredients. Most of the salads can be prepared in 10 minutes and most are measured for two. Each recipe combines Superfoods ingredients that deliver astonishing amounts of antioxidants, essential fatty acids (like omega-3), minerals, vitamins, and more.

Superfoods Today Kettlebells is a Kindle Kettlebells beginner's aimed at 30+ office workers who want to improve their health and build stronger body without fat.

Superfoods Today Red Smoothies is a Kindle Superfoods Smoothies with more than 40 Red Smoothies.

Superfoods Today 14 Days Detox is a Kindle Superfoods Detox that gives you 2 week Superfoods Detox meal plan and recipes for Detox success.

Superfoods Today Yellow Smoothies is a Kindle Superfoods Smoothies with more than 40 Yellow Smoothies.

Superfoods Today Green Smoothies is a Kindle Superfoods Smoothies with more than 35 Green Smoothies.

Superfoods Today Purple Smoothies is a Kindle Superfoods Smoothies with more than 40 Purple Smoothies.

Superfoods Cooking For Two is a Kindle that contains over 150 Superfoods recipes for two created with 100% Superfoods ingredients.

Nighttime Eater is a Kindle that deals with Nighttime Eating Syndrome (NES). Don Orwell is a life-long Nighttime Eater that has lost his weight with Superfoods and engineered a solution around Nighttime Eating problem. Don still eats at night✎. Don't fight your nature, you can continue to eat at night, be binge free and maintain low weight.

Superfoods Today Smart Carbs 20 Days Detox is a Kindle Superfoods that will teach you how to detox your body and start losing weight with Smart Carbs. The book has over 470+ pages with over 160+ 100% Superfoods recipes.

Superfoods Today Vegetarian Salads is a Kindle that contains over 40 Superfoods Vegetarian Salads recipes created with 100% Superfoods ingredients. Most of the salads can be prepared in 10 minutes and most are measured for two.

Superfoods Today Vegan Salads is a Kindle that contains over 30 Superfoods Vegan Salads recipes created with 100% Superfoods ingredients. Most of the salads can be prepared in 10 minutes and most are measured for two.

Superfoods Today Soups & Stews is a Kindle that contains over 70 Superfoods Soups and Stews recipes created with 100% Superfoods ingredients.

Superfoods Desserts is a Kindle Superfoods Desserts with more than 60 Superfoods Recipes.

Smoothies for Diabetics is a Kindle that contains over 70 Superfoods Smoothies adjusted for diabetics.

50 Shades of Superfoods for Two is a Kindle that contains over 150 Superfoods recipes for two created with 100% Superfoods ingredients.

50 Shades of Smoothies is a Kindle that contains over 70 Superfoods Smoothies.

50 Shades of Superfoods Salads is a Kindle that contains over 60 Superfoods Salads recipes created with 100% Superfoods ingredients. Most of the salads can be prepared in 10 minutes and most are measured for two. Each recipe combines Superfoods ingredients that deliver astonishing amounts of antioxidants, essential fatty acids (like omega-3), minerals, vitamins, and more.

Superfoods Vegan Desserts is a Kindle Vegan Dessert with 100% Vegan Superfoods Recipes.

Desserts **for Two** is a Kindle Superfoods Desserts with more than 40 Superfoods Desserts Recipes for two.

Superfoods Paleo Cookbook is a Kindle Paleo with more than 150 100% Superfoods Paleo Recipes.

Superfoods Breakfasts is a Kindle Superfoods with more than 40 100% Superfoods Breakfasts Recipes.

Superfoods Dump Dinners is a Kindle Superfoods with Superfoods Dump Dinners Recipes.

Healthy Desserts is a Kindle Desserts with more than 50 100% Superfoods Healthy Desserts Recipes.

Superfoods Salads in a Jar is a Kindle Salads in a Jar with more than 35 100% Superfoods Salads Recipes.

Smoothies for Kids is a Kindle Smoothies with more than 80 100% Superfoods Smoothies for Kids Recipes.

Vegan Cookbook for Beginners is a Kindle Vegan with more than 75 100% Superfoods Vegan Recipes.

Vegetarian Cooking for Beginners is a Kindle Vegetarian with more than 150 100% Superfoods Paleo Recipes.

Foods for Diabetics is a Kindle with more than 170 100% Superfoods Diabetics Recipes.

Made in the USA
San Bernardino, CA
18 July 2017